Show Up and Bring Coffee

How to Support Your Friends With Disabled Children

Megan Amrich

Show Up and Bring Coffee

How to Support Your Friends With Disabled Children

ISBN: 979-8-9886726-0-9 (Paperback)

ISBN: 979-8-9886726-1-6 (Hardcover)

ISBN: 979-8-9886726-2-3 (Ebook)

"In hard times, people don't want to be told to look on the bright side. They want to know you're on their side. Even if you can't help them feel better, you can always help them feel seen. The best way to support others is not to cheer them up. It's to show up."

- Adam Grant

TABLE OF CONTENTS

INTRODUCTION

"The next time we get into this car, we will be completely different people. We will be parents."

I remember thinking this as my husband Chris and I pulled into the hospital parking lot. It was late 2016, and we were arriving for my scheduled labor induction. I knew that once my son, JB, was born, our lives would be forever changed. I never could have predicted just how accurate that would be.

From the day he was born, there were health concerns about JB's feeding, weight, and developmental milestones (or lack thereof). By the time JB was six months old, he had already been hospitalized three separate times, undergone major surgery, and amassed a team of medical specialists across our state. He was completely dependent on a feeding tube (G tube) for all of his nutrition. We later learned that JB had a rare genetic syndrome that caused, among other things, lack of muscle tone, feeding issues, developmental delays, and seizures.

As I write this, JB is now a silly, sassy kindergartner. He especially loves participating in music class, joining his friends for circle time, and riding around on his tricycle. His life may look different from his peers, but he continues to amaze us with his resilience.

It feels strange to tell our story now, as if I'm almost watching a movie of the ups and downs of the past six years. These have been the most difficult, and most rewarding, years of my life so far. Our family has experienced trauma and growth, terrifying hospital stays, and jubilant milestones. Like the saying goes, "The days are long, but the years are short."

What makes me an expert on supporting parents of disabled children? To be honest, it is the incredible group of loved ones who have shown compassion and kindness every step of the way during my family's journey these past six years. Their example has inspired me to share my own experiences so that if you have people in your lives who may be dealing with their child's disability or medical diagnosis, you will feel more empowered to show up for them.

What does it mean to show up?

The good news is, just by reading this book, you're already taking the first step of showing up!

Showing up is taking time out of your busy life to ease your loved one's challenges. It's being fully present and acknowledging someone else's experiences. There are so many different ways you can show up for someone. We're going to talk about many examples throughout this book.

Obviously, people have their own lives and responsibilities, so doing everything suggested in this book will be impossible. My intention is for you to find a few tips that speak to you and your life. You can then put those tips into practice when your loved one is having a particularly difficult time. If you are a parent of a disabled child, I hope you can find some inspiration for ways to ask your village to help out along the way before you become overwhelmed or desperate.

Why this book is different

There are a lot of books out there for parents or guardians of disabled, medically complex, and/or neurodivergent children. (Visit joyfulbraveawesome.com/resources for some of my favorites.) What isn't out there, however, is a book about how to support those caregivers.

This makes no sense!

Chances are, at some point, every one of us will know someone whose life is altered by a child's diagnosis. Unicef reports that internationally there are almost 240 million children (ages 0 to 17) with at least one disability. In North America, approximately 1 in 10 children is disabled.

The US Center for Disease Control reports even greater numbers, with 1 in 6 children (ages 3 to 17) having at least one developmental disability. (Statistics vary due to varying definitions of what falls under disability.)

Odds are that even if you do not have a disabled child, you know someone—in your friend group, family, office, house of worship, neighborhood—who does or will. It's guaranteed that person could probably use an extra set of hands or a reassuring word every now and then.

Even those with disabled children can use advice on how to support others. Just as the challenges and characteristics of each illness or disability are different, so are everyone's strengths, weaknesses, and areas of need. It's good to have as many tools as possible in our supportive friend toolkits!

What to expect in this book

This book is broken down into nine chapters, each focused on a specific category of advice to keep in mind so you can better understand and support a friend. They are:

1. Listen without dismissing.

2. Be knowledgeable, not a know-it-all.

3. Offer an extra set of hands.

4. Behold the power of food and drink!

5. Familiarize yourself with feeding tubes.

6. Set an example of inclusion and acceptance for your own children.

7. Follow your friend's lead.

8. Recognize your friend as more than a caregiver.

9. Hold space for grief.

Some chapters include suggestions for tangible, immediate ways to help your friend. Other chapters deal with the emotional support aspect of helping.

Throughout this book, you'll find personal anecdotes from my own experiences as the mother of a disabled child. Some of these stories I have previously reflected upon in my blog—*Joyful, Brave & Awesome*—while others I am sharing for the first time.

I personally learn better by making connections between what I am reading and other things I may have seen or heard. As a result, I'm going to be using many examples from pop culture—specifically TV shows from the past decade or so—to illustrate concepts in this book. You'll see these labeled, "As seen on TV."

I've also included some additional information on topics readers may be less familiar with—tube feeding, adaptive fashion, and inclusive playgrounds/attractions. These sections are titled, "In case you were wondering."

Each chapter will end with "Say this" and "Do this" lists. These are NOT exhaustive lists, but are great jumping-off points for those looking to initiate helpful conversations or actions.

A note about language

I will be using the term "disabled" throughout this book. I will not be using "special needs" unless I am directly quoting someone. I am also including medically complex and neurodivergent people when I say "disabled" as people often fall into several of these groups.

When discussing neurodiversity, specifically autism, I will be using identity-first language (autistic person) rather than person-first language (person with autism).

I realize there are many schools of thought about language, ableism, and representation. My intention is to respect and use the language most commonly preferred by disabled and neurodivergent self-advocacy groups. For more information regarding language and disability, I highly recommend Emily Landau's book *Demystifying Disability*.

Okay, now that all of that is out of the way, let's get started!

Chapter 1:
Listen Without Dismissing

"Let me hold the door for you. I may have never walked in your shoes, but I can see your soles are worn, your strength is torn under the weight of a story I have never lived before."
- Morgan Harper Nichols

Everyone needs a friend like Leanne.

Leanne and I met in Pennsylvania when we lived in apartments across from each other. We've stayed in touch ever since.

During our last year as neighbors, Leanne was fighting to get answers regarding her young son's health and developmental delays. To this day, she is one of the strongest parents/advocates I've ever known.

When JB was a few months old, he was losing weight and failing to meet milestones. I called Leanne. "Something is different. I know it," I said. I then shared that many of JB's behaviors were similar to what we had seen in her son, who was later diagnosed as autistic.

It felt like everyone was telling me I was imagining things. They said I was worrying too much (which, to be fair, I do), that JB was just a bit behind, and he seemed "perfectly normal." He couldn't have anything "wrong" with him. Even suggesting the possibility was too scary for them to admit. (Looking back, I realize how ableist much of this language is. I am using it in this context only to better represent my experience at the time.)

Leanne did not say this, however. She listened to my concerns and calmly said, "There could be many different explanations. Yes, autism could be a part of it. But regardless of the diagnosis, I will be with you, and we will do this together. You have me."

Someone finally heard me and rather than changing the subject or dismissing me, told me that I had their unconditional support.

My biggest fear—that my child was different—was not actually catastrophic, despite what others' discomfort and avoidance suggested. Leanne's family was proof of this.

Toxic positivity and the backhanded compliment of "special people"

Heather Lanier is the author of the book *Raising a Rare Girl: A Memoir*, chronicling her daughter Fiona's first five years. In the book, Lanier describes how loved ones often corrected her when she said "if" instead of "when" in talking about her daughter's future. Such as "if she talks."

"People rewrote my sentiment with a single word—when. 'You mean, when she walks.' I understood their intentions: They believed in the power of positive thinking. But plenty of kids with Wolf-Hirschhorn syndrome [the syndrome Fiona has] didn't walk or talk, and it wasn't because their parents hadn't believed."

Positivity and optimism do have their place, don't get me wrong. But they can also be empty sentiments we share when we are uncomfortable and don't know what else to say. They can become toxic quickly, especially when used to shut down someone sharing their story.

Brené Brown is a researcher and bestselling author who specializes in, among other things, vulnerability and empathy. In her 2021 book *Atlas of the Heart*, she explains common misconceptions surrounding what empathy is and is not:

"We need to dismiss the myth that empathy is 'walking in someone else's shoes,'" she writes. "I need to learn how to listen to the story you tell about what it's like in your shoes and believe you even when it doesn't match my experiences."

One of the most common platitudes parents of disabled children hear is "God only gives special kids to special people." I was talking with a friend about how much I genuinely hate the phrase. She said that when someone says the phrase they are saying it is okay for you to have hardships because you are different and magically able to handle challenges better than other people. By this logic, they're saying they aren't "special," and they won't ever have to deal with challenges in their lives. This isn't a compliment. It's a way to separate themselves from you and minimize your suffering.

Statements like "God only gives special kids to special people" aren't coming from a place of empathy. Rather, they stem from sympathy and pity, which Brown says are, "the emotions of: We feel bad for you. From way over here where the kind of misery you're experiencing doesn't happen."

At least: My least favorite words

Look on the bright side. At least . . .

Ah, the dreaded "at least." Admit it, we've all heard, and probably said "at least" phrases before. Some common ones parents of disabled kids often hear are:

- At least it wasn't inherited.

- At least doctors diagnosed this early.

3

- At least she doesn't look sick.

- At least he's too young to remember all the hospitalizations and testing.

- At least it's not degenerative.

- At least you don't have other kids you have to juggle.

- At least you are able to be a stay-at-home parent.

- At least they seem happy.

To quote Brené Brown yet again, "Rarely, if ever, does an empathetic response begin with 'at least.'"

Why are these two words so harmful, regardless of your intentions? This phrase is always followed by a reason why someone shouldn't complain, why others have it worse, why the other person has no right to be upset. Simply put: It's shaming disguised as optimism.

When we are experiencing difficult emotions, the last thing we need is to be shamed. Trust me, we are often already shaming ourselves. What we do need is a safe space to share feelings, with no fear of judgment or interruption.

Psychologist Joanna Griffin describes this need for unconditional support in her book *Day by Day: Emotional Wellbeing in Parents of Disabled Children*. "Often parent carers require a safe space to voice their difficulties (particularly a current battle or challenge)," she writes. "This beautifully illustrates the arc of the parent career path—we need to be allowed to process the negatives to get to the positives."

As seen on TV: *Parks & Recreation*

In one of my favorite *Parks & Recreation* episodes, the character Ann Perkins (Rashida Jones) gets frustrated when her boyfriend

Chris Traeger (Rob Lowe) meets all of her pregnancy complaints with perkiness, upbeat sayings, or relentless optimism. She wants to vent about her swollen ankles, her exhaustion, her indigestion, but he just wants to focus on the power of positivity and nutritional supplements. Ann's friends finally tell Chris to stop trying to fix problems and instead say the two magic words Ann's really looking to hear: "That sucks."

I love this example because Chris is not intentionally trying to dismiss Ann's experience or comments. He is genuinely trying to support her by offering inspirational messages and well meaning, albeit overly eager, advice. I don't think anyone points out the silver lining in a situation with ulterior motives in mind. We, like Chris Traeger, are trying earnestly to alleviate loved ones' discomfort.

On the other hand, we all want someone, Rob Lowe or not, to say, "That sucks!" sometimes. We want someone to just listen to us vent for just a few minutes about how unfair everything is.

Say this:

- I'm here for you, no matter what.

- I don't know what to say, but I am listening.

- That sucks.

Do this:

- Listen.

Chapter 2:
Be knowledgeable, not a know-it-all

Two weeks before JB's first birthday, we received a call from his geneticist. The test results were in, and we had a diagnosis. JB had a rare genetic syndrome that caused low muscle tone, feeding issues, developmental delays, and seizures.

At the time of JB's diagnosis, there was no name for his specific syndrome, but rather a series of letters and numbers indicating the chromosomal location of the genetic difference. It looked like a license plate number, or one of those randomly generated passwords suggested by your browser.

While there is now a name for JB's specific syndrome, I prefer not to share it. The main reason is out of respect for JB's privacy. This is his story to tell someday if he chooses. The other reason I rarely share JB's diagnosis is because I don't want people jumping to conclusions or assuming they are suddenly experts based on the very limited information and research available.

Your friend is the expert when it comes to their child, their child's diagnosis, and the daily tasks required to provide that child the best possible care. This is because when you're the parent of a child with complex medical needs, you suddenly need to have the knowledge equivalent to advanced degrees in nursing, genetics, biochemistry, and more.

Not-so-fun fact: It turns out that when your friend's child starts seeing a new physician, that friend is expected to inform the doctor of the ins and outs about their child's syndrome and present them with the pertinent academic research on the specific condition. During ER visits and hospital stays, that friend may have to repeatedly explain their child's syndrome to different medical personnel, especially if it is a teaching hospital.

While this is daunting, to say the very least, it also means your friend has plenty of practice explaining their child's diagnosis. If you have questions, or would like to learn more, be honest and ask your friend. Just be sure to let them know you want to respect their privacy and understand if they don't want to talk about their child's health. Also ask if there are specific, trustworthy websites they recommend for you to research and learn more on your own. NEVER ask if your friend's child will grow out of it, if they are sure they got the right diagnosis, or what their child's life expectancy is.

Trust your friend, not Facebook

If the pandemic taught us anything, it is that some people will believe almost anything they read online, even finding their random sources more credible than actual medical based information.

Just because you saw something while scrolling through social media, it does not mean you know more about certain aspects of that care, such as nutrition, therapies, or medication. You obviously love your friend and trust them to be part of your life in a meaningful way. Now trust their judgment as a parent.

To put it more bluntly: The girl who sat behind you in your high school English class who now sells essential oils does NOT know more about your friend's son's gastrointestinal system than your friend does. So feel free to support your former classmate's small business if you'd like, but respect your friend when they say they're going to stick with their son's existing reflux medication, thank you very much.

Shaming with "should"

If you've ever brought home a new baby or puppy, you've no doubt gotten a lot of unsolicited advice from friends, family and even total strangers. You should try this sleep training method, or this food, or this pediatrician/veterinarian. Some of this advice may have been helpful, but the majority of it probably went in one ear and out the other. There is no way you could follow every piece of advice you receive those first few months!

Since JB started having health problems, it's been very much like that scenario. We should switch all of his local healthcare providers to doctors in a bigger city instead. We should fight harder for more testing or resources. We should be applying for grants, buying that special toy, making these home accessibility improvements, or taking him to more therapies.

There is a common stereotype for mothers (never fathers) as warrior moms or mama bears—advocates who go in, guns blazing, to every meeting or appointment ready to take names and kick butt. This portrayal plays a big part in people's expectations of moms with sick kids.

People tend to mean well in these circumstances. They just want to help in some way. But just like during the newborn phase, there is no way one set of parents can do everything.

Saying, "You should rest!" is not helpful. It only adds to parents' never-ending to-do lists. Never say, "You need to take time for yourself" or something like it without ALSO including an action you will personally take to make that break or self-care time possible. For example: "You need a break. I'll watch the kids tomorrow. You can get a manicure, sleep, or whatever you'd like to do for the afternoon." Or try this: "Here's a Domino's gift card. Order delivery tonight and use that time you'd be cooking to do something for yourself."

If you remember nothing else in this entire chapter, remember this: **Parents of disabled/medically complex children are drowning in "should," so they have to pick their battles carefully.**

That may mean staying with their doctors because they are geographically closer to their home, even if they may not rank as high on some national list. That may mean stopping after the third appeal to the health insurance company, and not fighting with the state board for coverage on this treatment. That may mean postponing toilet training for another year or two because there are only so many hours in a day. It does NOT mean that they are lazy, or quitters, or giving up on their child. They are focusing their limited energy and resources on what see as the greatest priority at the current moment. They can be warriors, but they must be strategic about when, where, and how.

Say this:

- Are there specific websites/resources you've found helpful in learning more about your child's syndrome/condition?

Do this:

- Trust your friend's judgment.

- Ditch the "should."

- If you want to learn more about a certain condition or health topic, seek out reputable, trustworthy sources.

Chapter 3:
Offer an extra set of hands

One of the greatest things a loved one can say to me is, "Can you show me how to operate JB's feeding pump? I'd love to be able to help out."

Seriously, it doesn't get much better than that. Okay, maybe, "I've brought your celebrity crushes John Krasinski and Trevor Noah here to join you for an evening of boy band karaoke and ice cream sundaes," is better, but the offer to help is a VERY close second.

As mentioned in chapter 2, parents of disabled children undergo trial by fire when it comes to learning about their children's conditions, equipment, and medical needs. After all, no one teaches them what to expect at an IEP meeting or how to calculate feeding pump rates in their heads while working on two hours of sleep. It often just feels necessary to keep doing everything on their own rather than train someone else to help.

"I think there's a huge need for close loved ones to step in and to take care of that child if possible," says Madeline Cheney, founder of *The Rare Life* podcast for parents of medically complex children. "Some of us still aren't at the point where we will be able to trust that because we're still so protective of our children and taking in consideration all of their medical needs. But a lot of us are."

11

Do you want to take on a greater role in helping your friend with medical-related tasks?

Be honest and open about your desire to learn more about how you can help. Mention that you want to be able to offer an extra set of hands and you know there may be a learning curve, but you are willing to try.

"I promise you that we will be the most understanding teachers. We 100% understand how overwhelming and scary it feels at first, because we were there," says Cheney.

Here's a brief list of medical or equipment-related things you could ask to help with. Obviously not all apply in every case, but maybe there are one or two that stick out to you:

- Operate the feeding pump.

- Give him his medicines.

- Get her ready for bed.

- Do his therapy exercises with him.

- Fold/unfold their wheelchair.

- Monitor her insulin.

- Position them in their stander/gait trainer.

- Mix his formula.

- Calm her when she's overstimulated.

- Use their nebulizer.

- Turn on his iPad/tablet/AAC device.

- Wash supplies.

- Change diapers.

Ask if there is a particular task that would be most helpful for you to learn. Maybe your friend wants you to know how to operate the feeding pump so you can stay with their child while they take a half hour nap. Or perhaps they want you to review the bedtime routine and all that entails, so they can go out on a date with their spouse for the first time in six months.

Don't be surprised if you get some push back along the lines of, "Don't worry about it. It's easier if I just do it." It doesn't mean they don't appreciate the offer. And it doesn't mean they won't take you up on it another time. Keep asking.

Ew, medical stuff

I get it, I get it. Many people just cannot deal with medical-related stuff. I was one of those squeamish people until I had JB. Whether it's due to past trauma or a sensitive stomach, if you don't think you can handle helping your friend with certain medical tasks, be honest. Chances are your friend already realizes this. Making yourself gag or get sick will only make things worse in an already tough situation.

Instead, think of tasks that you're comfortable doing to assist your friend. You know, the day-to-day housework that, as Cheney puts it, "understandably goes on the total backburner or off the whole stove completely" during especially stressful times like hospital stays.

Some of the items you can check off your friend's to-do list, whether yourself or by hiring someone else, include:

- Shoveling/plowing.

- Yardwork.

- Laundry.

- Taking out trash/recycling.

- Bringing car to get oil change.

- Pet-sitting.

- Swinging by post office/UPS.

- Bringing in mail.

And don't forget to ask how you can help with your friend's other children. As Cheney says, "Having another child in the family that is non-disabled adds a whole other layer of overwhelm to our already full plates because we need to take care of that child. And we're aware of all the ways that their siblings' disabilities affect them."

As seen on TV: *The Office*

The Office is my favorite TV show of all time. In the season 4 episode "Benihana Christmas," there is a scene where Dwight Schrute is upset because he's seated at the opposite end of the table from his boss/friend, Michael Scott. Michael has just been dumped, and Dwight wants to support him through this difficult time.

"How can I be *there* for Michael when I'm *here* for Michael?" Dwight asks.

I absolutely love this quote. It shows how often we take the phrase "being there" literally.

During the pandemic, people had to learn and adjust to almost all relationships being long distance. Geographic location was no longer a valid excuse for not being able to participate. Thanks to technology, any home could become a classroom, family reunion, doctor's office, fine dining establishment, zoo, and concert hall.

You may not be next-door neighbors with your friend, but that doesn't mean you're absolved from showing up. Don't let physical location be a barrier to emotional presence.

Here's a partial list of ways you can be there for your friend, whether an hour away or a hemisphere away:

- Hire someone to help with any of the household tasks mentioned in the previous list.

- Send e-gift cards to retailers like Target, Walmart, etc. (See chapter 7 for more financial-related ideas.)

- Send restaurant gift cards. (See chapter 4 for more food-related ideas.)

- Help with administrative tasks like proofreading emails, making phone calls, or ordering supplies.

Say this:

- What tasks (medical or otherwise) can I help with that would be the biggest benefit to you right now?

- Can you show me how to operate your child's feeding pump (or other equipment) so I can babysit this weekend?

Do this:

- See the lists above. Pick out a few of your favorite suggestions and get to work!

Chapter 4:
Behold the power of food and drink!

"Social protocol states when a friend is upset, you offer them a hot beverage." - Sheldon Cooper, The Big Bang Theory

I have never been so excited to see Lunchables, not even in the 1990s when they were at the peak of coolness.

Okay, let me back up a bit.

It was January 2018, and JB was in the hospital recovering from a particularly terrible virus. Because our local hospital's PICU (pediatric intensive care unit) was full at the moment, JB was transported to a hospital an hour away.

It just so happened that a close friend of mine had recently started working in the same city as this hospital. When she heard about JB, she immediately texted and said she was coming. Sure enough, she battled evening rush hour traffic to bring us an assortment of celebrity gossip magazines, candy, and Lunchables. It was the perfect mix of nostalgia and practicality to keep our spirits up after one of the scariest 24 hours of our parenting life.

Hospitals: Where time is a blur and food is an afterthought

Food has the ability to comfort people almost instantly, whether it's prepackaged cheese and crackers, or a complete Thanksgiving dinner. Hospital cafeteria food has its good points, namely, convenience, but there is something so re-energizing about a change in routine during the "time has lost all meaning" vortex of a child's hospitalization.

"When you're in the thick of appointments and hospitalizations, and just kind of processing trauma, like something so basic as 'what are we going to eat?' feels so overwhelming," says Madeline Cheney.

For Cheney, it was a gift of dried mangoes that sticks out most in her mind. "We had just gotten home from the hospital and had received devastating news about our son," she says. "Out of the blue a friend of mine texted me and said, 'Hey, I'm going to the store. Is there anything I can grab you?' I just started crying and thought, 'I feel seen right now. I feel like someone is there for me when I feel so alone.' There was nothing we needed like eggs or milk, so I said, 'Yes, please bring me dried mangoes, because that's a comfort food I have,' and she did. She had two little kids, and it wasn't easy for her, but she did that, and it was a hug. It was love. It just meant so much to me."

If your loved one has a child in the hospital, or is just coming home from a hospital stay, food is probably one of the last things on their mind. Here are some ways you can help—after asking about any dietary restrictions, allergies, or preferences:

- Bring them takeout from their favorite restaurant to the hospital.

- Coordinate and create a meal train or sign up on an existing meal train.

- Send an electronic gift card for pizza, or for a delivery service like GrubHub, DoorDash, or UberEats.

- Offer to grocery shop for them and restock their fridge when they return home.

- Don't forget the pets! See if you can pick up some food for their animals.

- Double the recipe when cooking for your own family. It requires almost no extra time to make double the food. Just be sure to use disposable containers, so your friend doesn't have to worry about washing and returning your serving dish.

As seen on TV: *The Big Bang Theory*

(In this section, I'm going to be saying coffee a lot, but know you can substitute it for tea, chai, cocoa, whatever—caffeinated or not, hot or iced—in your head while reading. It doesn't matter what the beverage, just the message behind it.)

On the sitcom *The Big Bang Theory*, main character Sheldon Cooper frequently reminds people that it is customary to offer someone a hot beverage if they are in distress. Over the 12 seasons of the series, we see him offer a warm beverage to people time and time again, even when he's being otherwise insensitive to (or unaware of) what his friends are going through.

It's no surprise that I love coffee. I mean, it's in the title and on the front cover of this very book, and a to-go cup is part of my blog logo. For me, coffee equals comfort, a sense of feeling safe and secure. Growing up, we only had coffee brewing in our house if our grandparents were visiting or if we were hosting a big event, like a holiday or graduation party. So, of course, I learned from an early age to love the smell of coffee, because it meant spending special time with loved ones.

When I was brainstorming ideas for this book, I kept returning to Sheldon's insistence on always offering a hot beverage to someone who was sad. I think it's difficult to know where to start in helping someone. We may be like Sheldon, and not know what to say, do, or how to make the situation better.

19

One of the simplest ways you can show your friend you are there for them is by asking if they want a coffee each time you are on your way to visit. It can be a simple text: "Hey, swinging by the coffee shop. What do you want?" You can save a note in your phone of their go-to order at Dunkin'. You can even just send them a gift card and say something like, "Breakfast is on me today!" Make it a habit: If you're showing up, bring coffee.

If you are nearby and have a bit more time, ask your friend if they want to meet up for coffee sometime. Be creative with the location if you have to. My friends and I have had coffee dates in my garage, in backyards, in parking lots, and in hospital visitor lounges.

Say this:

- What's your go-to coffee order?

- I'm bringing you dinner tomorrow night. Does anyone in your family have food allergies/dietary restrictions I should be aware of?

- Do you have a favorite local restaurant?

Do this:

- Pick a suggestion or two above that would work best for your friend's circumstances. Surprise them with a meal, snack or beverage this week!

Chapter 5:
Familiarize yourself with feeding tubes

What? An entire chapter devoted to the topic of feeding tubes. After all, only some children use feeding tubes. Well, until I became a "tubie mom" for JB, I had no idea this world even existed. If a loved one told me their child was getting a feeding tube placed, I would have thought it was a death sentence, and I would have done a terrible job pretending otherwise.

When I first heard the gastrointestinal (GI) doctor say JB needed a feeding tube, I thought it meant JB would need to live in a hospital. After all, until then every image I had ever seen of someone with a feeding tube involved a person lying in a hospital bed, asleep or comatose, and hooked up to a tangle of wires and monitors.

Thankfully, the GI doctor, along with a nurse and a nutritionist, explained how common tube feeding (also known as enteral feeding) actually is. "Tubies," or people that use feeding tubes, live fulfilling lives going to school, playing sports, making friends, having careers, and raising families. Their tubes simply provide them the nutrition and energy to participate in these activities.

If kindergartners can deal with it, so can you!

It's funny, but there are two different, and totally appropriate, reactions kids typically have when they learn about JB's feeding tube:

21

1. The kid shrugs and says, "Oh," and moves on to another topic or walks away. My favorite example of this was when a friend's daughter literally said, "Oh. I'm going to check on my worm now. Bye."

2. The kid says, "Oh," and then asks an amazing follow-up question like, "Does he drink Magic Formula like Boss Baby?" In case you were wondering the same thing, yes, JB gets a specific, special formula, and I guess it's kind of magic because it gives him all of his needed nutrition. But he doesn't drink it with his mouth in a bottle or cup.

JB's feeding pump is roughly the size of a Nintendo Switch (slightly larger than a Game Boy, for you fellow millennials). It really only draws attention when it beeps, a loud, high-pitched beep alerting you when his feed is done, there is a kink in the tubing, or sometimes seemingly for no reason at all. So imagine my delight when JB's kindergarten teacher told us that by the second month of school, his fellow students no longer reacted when his pump beeped in class. "They either ignore it, or say, 'JB is done eating!' and go about their activities," she said.

It took almost no time for these classmates to be unfazed by JB's pump. That's why I know it is possible for adults, too.

It doesn't have to be awkward

Okay, so what can you do for your friend that has a child using a feeding tube? There are several different ways you can help. If your friend and their family are at your house, just act like you would if your friend were breastfeeding or bottle feeding their child:

- Don't require them to do the feeding in another room, but offer the option if they prefer privacy.

- If their child is in the middle of a feed, don't stare or gawk. Same goes for if the child spits up or vomits.

- Ask if there's anything they'd like you to have on hand, like bottled water. Also, ask if they need anything refrigerated (like formula or medication).

If you're planning an event, or it's a holiday where candy and treats are prevalent, consider incorporating some non-food treats into the line-up. Stickers, glow sticks, temporary tattoos, fidgets, and Play-Doh are great alternatives to candy. Plus, you won't have to worry about food allergies!

If you're having a party and you aren't sure if your friend's child will be eating or not, feel free to ask beforehand. Many tubies are able to eat by mouth. For example, my son can have small bites of purees or dissolvable snacks, and small sips of water. When JB attended his first friend birthday party last year, I almost cried when I saw applesauce pouches among the other snacks. Just knowing that JB could eat something with his friends meant so much to me!

The emotional implications of having a child with a feeding tube

As I mentioned in chapter 4, food and emotions are connected in many ways, good and bad. If your friend's child has a feeding tube or may have a feeding tube placed at some point, there is undoubtedly a giant tangled mess of emotions swirling around your friend's mind.

First of all, to get to the point where a feeding tube is needed in an infant or toddler, your friend's child was most likely diagnosed with something called "failure to thrive." Yes, that's a real medical term physicians use to describe a child who is not gaining weight, or is losing weight, due to inadequate nutrition.

Lauren Lowery is a life coach and podcaster specializing in helping mothers of disabled and medically complex children. In episode 35 of her podcast, *Overcome the Overwhelm*, she shares her experience after her son Leo received a feeding tube.

"I took failure to thrive to mean failure as a mom," she says. "Every time I would go to feed him, I would break down crying. Every part [of tube feeding] was a trigger... Seeing the syringes, priming the tubing, all of it was such a reminder."

If your friend is having a difficult time handling the emotions that can come with having a child with a feeding tube, please refer to chapter 1 on listening and chapter 9 on holding space for grief.

In case you're wondering: Feeding tubes

There are several kinds of feeding tubes, each named for where it enters the body and/or delivers food.

- NG tube (Nasal Gastric, as it enters the nose and goes down to the stomach) or NJ tube (Nasal Jejunum, as it enters the nose and goes down to the small intestine). These are usually temporary. They are what you often see on babies in the NICU, taped onto the child's cheek.

- GJ tube (Gastro Jejunal, as it has a port into the stomach and a port into the jejunum part of the small intestine) or J tube (Jejunal). These are for longer-term use and require surgery to place initially, and then an additional procedure under anesthesia every three months to replace the tube.

- G tube (G is for Gastric, as it goes directly to the stomach). This is the most common long-term type of feeding tube. The G-tube button looks like a combination of a post earring and the air vent you use to blow up a beach ball. The button is surgically inserted into the stomach, basically like piercing an ear, but in the stomach, and has a wider "post." The button stays with a "backing," a plastic bubble you inflate with a few milliliters of water. If the button comes out, you simply reinsert it and reinflate the bubble. If the button comes out and isn't reinserted within an hour or two, the hole closes up. To feed, an extension tube is attached to get the food into the body, whether by syringe, gravity or pump.

So what goes into these tubes? Well, it depends on each person's nutritional needs and lifestyle. Breast milk, traditional infant formula, specialized formula for all ages, or blended and pureed foods are all options for tube-fed diets. Often times, medicine and water are also given through the feeding tube.

Yes, it may seem strange and intimidating as there's a small machine plugged in to a child's stomach. Yet it makes that child's life possible.

Say this:

- Can I get you anything while you set up for your child's feed?

- Do you need anything refrigerated while you're visiting?

Do this:

- Include non-food prizes and treats when hosting events.

- Be aware of the emotional implications associated with having a child using a feeding tube.

Chapter 6:
Set an example of what it means to be inclusive

A few years ago, a friend reached out to me on Facebook with the sweetest message. She wanted to know if I had any recommendations for how she and her young children should best engage with kids with disabilities in a way that is respectful and supportive. The fact that parents want their children to know about and celebrate differences is so reassuring to me. It gives me hope that kids are becoming more accepting of, and comfortable with, people who are not exactly like them.

Same and different

My friends and I have the best luck explaining JB's disabilities in terms of showing kids what's different between them and JB, and what's the same. So, if a child asks why JB doesn't walk, we say, "His legs aren't strong enough to walk yet like you do, but he has this special chair that helps him get around. Isn't it cool how many ways there are to move and explore?"

If they point to JB's feeding tube, we say, "That's how he gets food in his belly. JB can't take bites, chew, and swallow with his mouth like you do, but this tube is how JB eats a meal. Isn't it amazing how many ways there are to eat?"

This way they see what's different, but also what they have in common.

The main thing is to explain there's nothing to be afraid of and kids with disabilities are still just that—KIDS. They enjoy dinosaurs, Disney movies, hockey, stickers, iPads, and everything else other kids do.

I know what you're thinking: "What if my child says/asks something embarrassing or inappropriate, though?" Have there been a few of these moments for us? Of course! Children don't have filters; they say exactly what they are thinking as they think it. But if we are constantly shushing them and discouraging them from asking questions, we are saying that curiosity is a bad thing, and disabilities are something shameful to ignore or sweep under the rug.

I've been so impressed over the past few years at just how many more children's toys, books, and television programs now feature neurodivergent and/or disabled characters. Visit joyfulbraveawesome.com/resources for a list of some of my favorite children's picture books that explain disabilities in easy, approachable language.

Plan a playdate!

If possible, schedule a playdate to familiarize your kids with your friend's children in a smaller, one-on-one setting first (as opposed to at a big party or event). After all, it's one thing to see a picture of a wheelchair or feeding tube in a book or YouTube video, but another to meet someone who uses one.

The initial meeting can take place in person or online. Zoom/FaceTime playdates can give friends and family a safe and manageable way to meet and get to know each other. Let your pets be part of it, too! Online meetings are a great option for germy times, like flu season, and for friends and family who live far away.

If planning an in-person playdate somewhere in the community, you may want to ask your friend if there's a specific place their family likes to visit. Chances are your friend already knows one or two attractions that meet their child's unique mobility, social, and sensory needs. (See "In case you're wondering" for more information.)

If you know of an attraction or activity that seems like it might be a good fit, run it by your friend first. Your friend can do additional research, if necessary, and will appreciate you taking an interest in accommodating their child's unique needs.

Here's the Story(land)...

I want to share an amazing experience I had last year while we were planning a trip to Storyland, a children's theme park in New Hampshire. It was going to be JB's first time going to a theme park, other than the one in our hometown, and we weren't sure if he'd be able to go on any rides or handle the experience.

I reached out to a couple of my college friends who had been to Storyland. They were incredibly helpful, going above and beyond what I expected. One friend sent photos she had taken on each ride, so I could see the level of head control/upper body strength required to sit safely. She also made me a list of which rides allowed strollers and/or wheelchairs. Another friend explained where the family restrooms and the feeding rooms were so I could plan where to change and feed JB. I don't think we would've had nearly as wonderful a time if it weren't for these friends and their assistance. Never underestimate the difference it can make to share your experience with others!

In case you are wondering: Inclusive spaces

What does it mean for an attraction to be truly inclusive? Aren't a wheelchair ramp and an accessible parking space enough? Before having JB, I sure thought so.

Here are four common inclusion and accessibility features that you can look for next time you visit a new place.

1. Sensory-friendly showtimes and/or attraction hours: During these times, places like museums, theaters, or concert halls reduce sudden changes in lighting and sound, and limit the amount of people in the venue. Participants are encouraged to move around and express themselves as they see fit, whether it's dancing in the aisles or stepping away into a designated quiet space to calm down and recharge. We attended a sensory-friendly performance with the Boston Symphony Orchestra, and it was one of the most beautiful live performances I've ever attended, in part because of the comfort and joy of everyone involved.

2. Bathroom accommodations: Changing tables are great for little ones, but what about when an older child, teen, or adult need to be changed? Adult changing spaces offer people privacy, and save caretakers' backs, when needing to address private toileting or medical needs. In addition, many places have switched away from automatic toilets, sinks, soap dispensers, and hand dryers, as these can be extremely upsetting to some neurodivergent people.

3. Design features that allow wheelchair users to participate fully: Many parks and museums have guardrails placed right at wheelchair users' eye level, making it hard for them to see or interact with the attractions. The New England Aquarium in Boston really gets its whole audience. The focal point is a central tank four floors tall, with floor to ceiling viewing windows, and a ramp spiraling around it. As a result, you can see the animals, and occasional scuba divers, from almost any angle, whether sitting or standing.

4. Playgrounds for all: A truly inclusive playground starts from the ground up. Literally. Some playground surface materials like wood or rubber mulch may be ADA-compliant, but they are not wheelchair friendly unless meticulously

maintained. Options like poured-in-place rubber, however, are wheelchair-friendly and require far less maintenance. Inclusive playgrounds also feature a wide variety of attractions and activities—musical components, activity panels, braille features, and wheelchair ride-on options—that appeal to and work for people of all ages and abilities.

The attention to these different details and changes add up to a big relief for parents. As Joanna Griffin says, "Finding places that are fully inclusive and welcoming to children with special needs… helps create a sense of community and acceptance. I notice my own stress levels, and that of other parents, being much lower when attending such events."

Say this:

- Do you mind if my child asks some questions about your child's feeding tube, wheelchair, etc.?

- Let's schedule a playdate! Is there a particular park your family enjoys?

- I noticed some new features at this attraction that I think may help your family on their next trip. When it works for you, let's get together so I can tell you all about them.

Do this:

- Add inclusive toys and books to your child's playroom and bookshelves.

- Support inclusive playground initiatives in your area.

- Think of how groups you belong to can make events and performances more inclusive.

Chapter 7:
Follow your friend's lead

I don't know your friend. (Unless that friend is me. In that case, you have fantastic taste in friends!) You, however, *do* know your friend. You know their personality, their likes and dislikes, their sense of humor, their favorite ice cream flavor, all the things.

So, in many ways, you already know how to comfort them.

Maybe your friend's love language is Italian pastry. Or group texts consisting entirely of *Friends* GIFs. Perhaps they have a dark sense of humor, or like listening to pop punk music when they are having a truly bad day.

Sometimes what a person needs isn't distraction, or talking about a problem, or advice. It can be tough to know exactly what to say or do.

When I don't know the right thing to say, I'm honest about it. I often just ask, "What would bring you the most comfort right now?" I truly listen to what they tell me and honor their request.

Timing is another important aspect when it comes helping a friend in the best, most needed way. If your friend is running from appointment to appointment with their child, texting may make the most sense. If they're at home with their child, phone calls may make the most sense, so your friend can talk on speaker and have their hands free to adjust tube feeds, change diapers, etc. Or maybe what your friend really wants is in-person adult interaction, whether it is meeting at a coffee shop or at home.

Tricky topics: Religion, politics, and money

There are some tricky topics regardless of whether or not your friend has a disabled child. I'm talking about the subjects we are taught from an early age not to bring up in what's considered polite conversation—religion, politics, and money.

Is your friend religious and open about their beliefs? If so, and you feel comfortable discussing faith, then by all means use that as a form of connecting with and helping them during this time. Invite them to a worship service, pray with them, or discuss faith-based books and songs that may provide comfort.

If your faith is an important part of your own life, but not your friend's, you can still feel free to pray for them in your own way.

But if your friend is not outspoken about their religion, has different beliefs than you, or has no beliefs, then:

NOW IS NOT THE TIME TO BRING IT UP OR TRY TO
CONVERT THEM.

Stop. Go back. Reread that previous sentence. I'll wait.

Politics is also a sticky subject. You may be wondering why I am even mentioning politics in this book. The reality is that political decisions shape almost every aspect of life as a parent of a disabled child. Health care, insurance, child care expenses, paid family leave, special education programs, accessibility: These are all topics that have an immediate impact on families with disabled children.

Some political issues are especially triggering for parents of disabled children. For example, during the 2022 U.S. Supreme

Court's overturning of Roe v. Wade, I really struggled. As political pundits spouted opinions about genetic testing, chromosomal abnormalities, family planning, and reproductive health, the trauma from my first few months of motherhood came flooding back to me. I was so fortunate that my friends, whether they have similar or different political views than I do, were supportive and listened to me during that period. And when I needed some space to gather my thoughts, to reflect rather than debate, they understood.

Simple rule of thumb: Do not bring up politics unless your friend brings it up first. If you have strong opinions on a certain political topic, please know that your friend may have a different take due to personal experience.

Financial concerns are also a major, but often unspoken, part of life as a parent of a disabled child. Many of the topics mentioned under politics—health care, insurance, paid leave, family planning, child care—can turn a family's finances upside down after a disability diagnosis.

It's natural to want to help a friend going through a difficult period financially. Think, however, before launching something public like a GoFundMe or other fundraiser on their behalf. Maybe your friend doesn't want their personal life or their child's health information shared publicly. Maybe there is something in their past or in their personality that makes money-related issues especially sensitive or complicated. Maybe a fundraising initiative or large cash donation would interfere with financial assistance they are already receiving.

There are different ways you can help your friend financially while still respecting their privacy:

- Venmo them or send them a check to use however they see fit.

- Offer to pay for someone to help with household tasks (see chapter 3).

- Ask for their child's clothing sizes and next time you order something online, add an adaptive clothing item or two for them into your cart. (See "In case you're wondering" at the end of this chapter for more information.)

- See if they'd like any toys/gear your children may have outgrown.

- Give gift cards for gas stations, groceries, meal delivery services, restaurants, Target/Walmart, coffee, etc. (See chapter 4 for more food-related gift card ideas.)

I have some big news…

There is another complicated situation that often comes up between friends. How do you handle sharing happy news, such as announcing you are pregnant or celebrating your typically-developing child's big accomplishment, without upsetting your friend or feeling like you're showing off?

This scenario is one of the most important times to follow your friend's lead. If your friend is going through a particularly strong wave of grief, or dealing with an immediate setback or crisis, wait for a better time to bring up your news. A more opportune moment will present itself; I promise.

When you do share your happy news, do not be alarmed if your friend does not respond immediately, or seems distant afterward. They are not necessarily mad or jealous; They love you and of course they want you and your family to be happy and experience every possible joy. Your friend may just need to take some time for self-preservation and process the crazy range of emotions going through their own mind.

And take heart. The fact you are even thinking about how your friend will take the news is a sign you are doing something right. Your friend is lucky to have you!

In case you're wondering: Adaptive fashion

I am a huge fan of adaptive fashion—so much so that I wrote an entire article about it in 2021 for the website *TriplePundit*!

What exactly is adaptive fashion? It is clothing, footwear, and accessories designed to meet the needs of those with disabilities. Some common features found in adaptive clothing include:

- Larger openings and simpler fasteners (magnets or Velcro) for those with limited dexterity and fine motor skills to dress themselves more easily.

- Abdominal access, which allows for feeding tubes (usually in a concealed layer of a top, like a hoodie pocket or a built-in camisole in a shirt).

- Wide-leg pants with adjustable sides to allow room for leg braces to be worn.

- Extended size ranges on items like bodysuits, onesies, or diaper-friendly clothing.

- Differently proportioned pants, a design crucial for making sitting in a wheelchair more comfortable.

- Flat seams/no seams and tag-free labels also limit sensory overload for those with sensitivities.

As recently as 10 years ago, adaptive children's clothing was only available if you could sew or hire a tailor. There were some small vendors available online on Etsy, but there was no economy of scale, so prices were high for families. After all, as any parent knows, kids outgrow and wear out clothes quickly!

Now, major retailers like Target, Kohl's, and JCPenney have brought adaptive clothing prices down to the same price point as their other offerings by using the same materials. Today, JB's clothes look just like his peers,' with bright colors, patterns, and fun characters. The only difference is his pant legs have Velcro on the sides to accommodate his leg braces, and his shirts have special hidden holes for his feeding tube to thread through.

Say this:

- What would bring you the most comfort right now?

- Is it better if I text/call you regularly to check in, or wait for you to reach out to me?

- I'm about to place an online order from Target. Want me to add anything for you?

Do this:

- When it comes to spiritual or financial support for your friend, think of ways you can quietly help while still respecting your friend's privacy and beliefs.

- If you have exciting news about your child/family, carefully consider the best time to share with your friend.

Chapter 8:
Recognize your friend as more than a caregiver

"I didn't want to be seen as 'just' a caregiver anymore, my only value tied up in what I did for other people."
- Kate Washington, Already Toast

When JB was 18 months old, he was hospitalized. During his stay, the doctor replaced his G tube with a GJ (see chapter 5 for more information on the difference between tubes). The good news was it worked! Unfortunately, the complexity of the new tube meant he could no longer attend daycare. I left my career to stay at home with him full time.

The shift from working in an office to staying at home for family reasons can be jarring for anyone, regardless of the circumstances. But I don't think I fully understood just how isolating it would feel for an extrovert like myself to have no one to chat with throughout the day.

JB's in-home therapists (through our state's Early Intervention program) were my only source of adult interaction during the day. They were so kind and amazing, but while I was so grateful for their presence, I also longed for conversation that didn't revolve around my child and his disability. I missed being referred to and thought of as "Megan" and not just "JB's mom."

We get by with a little help from our friends

After becoming parents, many of us face the dilemma of having less time to devote to friendships, while at the same time needing our people more than ever. This is even truer for parents of disabled children.

"As we have a child with a medical complexity or disability, things get flipped on their head. Our whole lives change," Madeline Cheney says. "So we get that it's hard to be able to relate in the same ways that we did before. And honestly we won't be able to have the same relationship we had before because ... so much is different, not just about our lives, but about us."

Joanna Griffin writes that some of the parents she interviewed for her book, "made the important point that by keeping hold of old friends it allowed them to retain a part of themselves that existed prior to having children. A chance to connect, talk, and switch off."

"For some," she adds, "their friends offered time away from anything special-needs related."

A few days after giving my notice at work and JB being discharged from the hospital, I headed to my 10-year college reunion, encouraged by my family to enjoy this time with my friends. I felt guilty for having a weekend away, but it ended up being one of the best decisions I made.

Throughout the weekend, my friends and I reminisced about our college days. We talked about what had changed, or remained the same, on campus, in our relationships, and in our lives over the past decade.

The reunion provided me with a much-needed reminder that my college friends loved me even before I became a mother. They would continue loving me moving forward, regardless of my employment status or whether my child could walk independently.

What we are worth

For many people—myself included—it is easy for self-worth to be tied to objective external factors: Grade point averages, salary bracket, the number on the scale, etc. So when the unexpected happens, suddenly the value we place on ourselves can go into freefall. Lauren Lowery describes this scenario in episode 43 of her *Overcome the Overwhelm* podcast:

> You are thrown into a crazy situation of being a mother to a child who has disabilities, where no one tells you the rules. You've never even heard of this genetic condition you were just told that your child has. You've never taken a child to physical therapy.... You don't know anything about feeding tubes or behavioral issues, and you honestly have no idea what you're doing. It doesn't feel like you are successful because how do you even know what 'successful' is? How can you win at a game when you don't even know what you're playing?

I often find myself tying my own worthiness to my son's health.

I've heard variations of "Keeping your son healthy is the most important thing" from the time of my first maternity appointment, long before we knew how true that would really be. When you are constantly reminded of this sentiment, it's easy to internalize it and tell yourself that it's true, that therefore your own wellbeing is not important.

At one point during the Fall/Winter of 2022, during the height of the "tripledemic" (as the media was calling the unprecedented rise in COVID, flu, and RSV cases), I remember texting a close friend. I told her, "It feels like my value is entirely wrapped up in my son's health right now. If he gets sick with any of these viruses, it will be completely my fault that I've dropped the ball and not done my one job, to protect him."

My friend replied, "I can see why it may feel that way, but I hope you know that it's not true." She then reminded me of some of my strengths completely outside of being a mother.

Please, remind your friends often that they are cherished and worthy as people in their own right, and not solely because they are parents.

How to celebrate your friend outside of their role as caregiver

So how can you remind your friend that they are so much more than "just" a caregiver, while also strengthening your friendship?

Here are some suggestions, based on ways my loved ones have supported me over the years:

- Be your friend's cheerleader for any non-kid news they share, like a new hobby, job prospect, or personal achievement. Did they make a new recipe that looks awesome? Celebrate that! Put together a cute new outfit? Hooray!

- Send a care package with fun little items like scented candles, cute stationery, snacks, or some handmade jewelry.

- Schedule a dinner, brunch, winery visit, slumber party, coffee date, or some other type of get-together.

- Plan a virtual viewing party. Many streaming services allow you to send a link to friends so you can synchronize watching a movie or TV show across many devices and locations. This is great for shows you've seen a million times already and can quote together.

- Create a playlist with favorite songs from your group's high school or college days.

Say this:

- How are you doing?

- Can your spouse stay with the kids some night this week so we can go out to dinner and catch up?

- I am so proud of you for taking up a new hobby!

- You matter! You are enough!

Do this:

- Try and find one or two of the suggestions in the list earlier in this chapter, and see if you can implement them this month.

AMRICH

Chapter 9:
Hold space for grief

There's a common misconception that caregivers of disabled kids are bitter and suffering from a martyr complex. Case in point: For this chapter, I started counting how many times this exact trope was used in the *Law & Order* universe over the past 30 years. I stopped counting after a dozen.

I believe what is often viewed as resentment is actually grief. Grief over the loss of how we expected parenthood to be. Grief over the milestones and experiences our family may never experience. Grief over the isolation we feel. Grief over the toll this life takes on our relationships, finances, family planning, and careers. Grief over the discomfort we see our children endure with each procedure or hospital stay.

We are often reluctant to share our grief because society tells us grief is only for death. Grieving when a child is alive? That is selfish, ungrateful, and frankly disrespectful. What an awful parent!

Grieving a child's disability or diagnosis does not mean a parent doesn't love their child. Rather, grief is a necessary part of the process of learning to love that child as they truly are rather than as we expected our parenting life to look like.

Be mindful of milestones

Developmental milestones have been some of the biggest triggers for my grief. There's no escaping them. Each pediatrician appointment for many months and years is filled with questions like, "Is s/he grasping toys? Is s/he making consonant and vowel sounds?" Social media feeds are filled with photos and videos of former classmates' and distant relatives' children taking first steps, saying something precocious, or even just eating snacks.

Even basic daily interactions can lead to tough moments. While I was picking JB up from school one afternoon, another child ran over to me and shouted, "Mommy!" (His mother and I were dressed similarly, so it was an easy mistake to make.) The seemingly minor incident had me in tears for the remainder of the day, as it was the first time I had ever heard a child call me "Mommy." Even writing about it a year later is making me tear up. I never realized how much I wanted to hear JB say my name until I heard this other child say it.

It's easy to say, "Just don't compare!" or "It doesn't matter what anyone else's kid is doing!" but these suggestions are not helpful when someone is dealing with the grief of a milestone that may never come.

Celebrate regardless of progress

So what is the best way to support a friend experiencing grief related to their child's disabilities?

First of all, whenever your friend shares something that their child is trying or doing for the first time, and they sound genuinely excited about it, celebrate with them. It may not seem like a big deal to you, but trust me, it is a huge deal to your friend and their child!

A quick note: Some parents of disabled kids like using the term "inchstones" as opposed to "milestones" to describe the small but significant steps of progress their children make. I don't personally use this word, because I feel like it's cutesy and unintentionally does the opposite and minimizes disabled kids' efforts. If your friend uses this term, though, feel free to use it.

Secondly, if you notice their child has made progress in some area—eating more, sitting up more, or even paying more attention to a book or toy—than the last time you saw them, mention it to your friend. Sometimes, it can be hard for parents to see the progress being made because they're too close, and are constantly with their child. Parents can always use an outsider's perspective on finding growth they may have overlooked.

There may be more times than not where there isn't any talk about progress, though. That is okay. As discussed in chapter 1, often the best way to support someone is to hear them out, and listen to their worries and feelings without judgment or attempts to fix anything.

And finally, celebrate your friend's child for who they are, rather than what they can or cannot do. As Heather Lanier notes in her book, people often share stories of loved ones overcoming disabilities, rather than living with disabilities. What she longed to hear someone say just once was, "Oh, genetic condition? You know, my nephew has a genetic condition, and he can't walk or talk or feed himself, and do you know what? He's awesome, a great man. If I'd heard that, I would have burst into tears of gratitude."

As seen on TV: *Bluey*

Let's talk about "Baby Race," one of my favorite episodes of the adorable animated Australian children's program *Bluey*. Chilli (aka Mum) tells her daughters the story of how Bluey learned to crawl. Chilli mentions it was—in her mind at least—like a baby race to see who would crawl or walk first among the other children in the playgroup. When Bluey wasn't crawling like the others, Chilli questions her own fitness as a mother. Another mom from their playgroup comes to visit with Chilli. This mom mentions she's still learning as she goes, and this is her ninth kid! No wonder she seems like she has it all figured out. She then assures Chilli, "You're doing great."

Chilli cries, the audience cries, basically everyone cries.

I love this episode because it addresses how easy it is to fall into the comparison trap, and the guilt that can result. When JB didn't meet milestones, I assumed it was my fault. Fortunately, my friends, family, and coworkers were fantastic and supportive, reminding me, "You're doing great!" when I needed it most.

Say this:

- I'm so happy to hear your daughter is liking her new music therapy class!

- I noticed your son is sitting up independently a lot more lately. That is fantastic!

- Your child has such a kind heart.

Do this:

- Sit with your friend in their grief, offering an ear to listen and shoulder to cry on.

- Celebrate victories big and small.

- Acknowledge the strengths you see in your friend and their child.

Conclusion

I'll be honest, I've rewritten this conclusion at least a dozen times. Why so many changes? Because every time I sit down to write, I feel differently about my journey as a parent of a disabled child.

I think this is appropriate, though. Like me, some days your friend also may feel fine. Other days, the weight of the unknown may feel almost overwhelming, as your friend wonders, "Will my child ever be able to live independently?" or "Who will care for them if something happens to me?"

During particularly trying times, like during hospital stays, we are running on adrenaline and are in sort of a survival mode. "It's when we get back home," says Madeline Cheney, "that our brains and our bodies are able to kind of process those things. We need you to continue to support us even after our child is discharged, certainly during hospitalizations, but afterwards as well."

More often than not, it's in the everyday moments that we can use our friends' support most.

Look, I get it. The day-to-day struggles aren't shiny or exciting. There may not be a big fundraiser, cute silicone awareness bracelets, or Facebook profile frames. But there is still a need.

I think back to a Facebook post I wrote on my private, personal page when JB was still an infant. We were in the thick of trying to find some answers and a diagnosis for JB, and I admitted how overwhelmed I was feeling. I wasn't looking for attention or anything, I just needed to vent.

Something incredible happened after I opened up that day. Friends, many of whom I hadn't talked to since high school or college, began reaching out to me and sharing their own stories. Some were dealing with their own children's diagnoses. Others had friends or family members who had feeding tubes or developmental delays. And others just wanted to let me know they were thinking of me, and they felt they needed to reach out.

In her book *Already Toast*, Kate Washington discusses the caregiving crisis in America, and why our current systems are not equipped to help those who really need support. She says that we need to begin viewing caregiving, whether for the young, elderly, disabled, as "a valuable social effort rather than a draining, private individual obligation."

One way we can shift our collective mindset is by helping those who are currently caregivers. After all, we will more than likely all care for loved ones at some point in our lives.

"Jumping into the fray to contribute, even if it feels awkward, helps lessen the isolation of caregiving and build up the more community-minded, connected ethos we need if real changes in care are ever to come," Washington says.

So, as a caregiver right now, what do I want? I want someone to listen when I'm having a rough day, to love my child for being exactly who he is, to chat with me about the latest celebrity gossip while helping me with my son's tube feed. In short, I want someone to show up.

Oh yeah, and I want them to bring coffee!

Acknowledgements

"All of us have special ones who have loved us into being."
- Fred Rogers

There is something so comforting about the idea that people can care so deeply they elevate their loved ones into the most authentic, capable versions of themselves.

Many people have loved "Megan the Author" into being, making this book possible.

I'd like to begin by thanking my family for their never-ending support. Chris, JB, Mom, Dad, Amy, Mike, Joshua, Brian, and Bridget—thank you all! Also, thanks to my grandparents, in-laws, aunts, uncles, and cousins for their assistance.

Thank you to my Providence College ladies. I am so blessed to have your constant loyalty, compassion, and wisdom. Forever Friars!

I'd like to give a big shout out to the ragtag group from Noho known as the Snoopers (among other things). So many examples in this book are things you ladies have done for me! Thanks for being my village.

I am so grateful for the friends I made in Pittsburgh. You stood by Chris and me when we needed you most. Thank you for assuring us things would work out.

To the women I've met over the years through groups and retreats like A Mother's Rest weekends in the Berkshires. Thank you for sharing your honesty, resilience, and perspective.

Thank you to the incredible creators and entrepreneurs I've met through the Momme community. You encouraged me to believe in my writing and in myself.

Special thanks to Keylonda, my publisher and cheerleader, and Melinda, the one who helped me distill my crazy jumble of ideas into what would become the concept for this book.

Finally, thank you to everyone who has purchased or read this book. I am absolutely delighted with the thought that all of you want to help families with disabled children feel more included and appreciated in society.

Work Cited

Epigraph:

Grant, Adam. @AdamMGrant, "In hard times..." *Twitter*, 29 November 2022. 2:46 p.m. https://twitter.com/AdamMGrant/status/1597678377741488128

Introduction:

"Children With Disabilities Overview." *UNICEF* February 2022. data.unicef.org/topic/child-disability/overview/

"Health Needs and Use of Services Among Children with Developmental Disabilities." *Centers for Disease Control and Prevention* 24 March 2022. www.cdc.gov/ncbddd/developmentaldisabilities/features/developmental-disabilities-among-us-children.html

Landau, Emily. *Demystifying Disability*. Ten Speed Press, 2021.

Chapter 1:

Nichols, Morgan Harper. @morganhnichols, "Empathy..." *Twitter,* 8 February 2018. 12:18 p.m. https://twitter.com/morganhnichols/status/961650431427452928

Lanier, Heather. *Raising a Rare Girl*. Penguin, 2020, pages 86-87.

Brown, Brené. *Atlas of the Heart*. Random House, 2021, pages 123-124.

Brown, Brené. "Brené Brown on Empathy." *YouTube,* uploaded by RSA, 10 December 2013, www.youtube.com/watch?v=1Evwgu369Jw.

Griffin, Joanna. *Day by Day: Emotional Wellbeing in Parents of Disabled Children.* Free Publishing Limited, 2021, page 124.

Ch. 2:

Lanier, page 202

Ch. 3:

Cheney, Madeline, host and publisher. "Tangible Ways to Support Parents of Disabled Children." *The Rare Life,* season 6, episode 104, 20 October 2022. therarelifepodcast.com/show-notes/ep-104-tangible-ways-support-parents-disabled-children-message-our-loved-ones.

Ch. 4:

Cheney

Ch. 5:

Lowery, Lauren, host and publisher. "Comfort Food, Emotions, and G-Tubes." *Overcome the Overwhelm for Special Needs Moms,* episode 35, 26 May 2022, podcast.app/overcome-the-overwhelm-for-special-needs-moms-p2478182/.

Ch. 6:

Griffin, p. 37

Ch. 7:

Amrich, Megan. "What Is Adaptive Clothing, and Why Are More Retailers Offering It for Children?" *TriplePundit*, 26 July 2021, triplepundit.com/story/2021/adaptive-clothing-retailers/725971 .

Ch. 8:

Washington, Kate. *Already Toast.* Beacon Press, 2021, Chapter 6 (eBook edition).

Cheney

Griffin, p. 146

Lowery, Lauren, host and publisher. "Worthiness and Burnout." *Overcome the Overwhelm for Special Needs Moms,* episode 43, 21 July 2022, podcasts.apple.com/us/podcast/43-worthiness-and-burnout/id1585428099?i=1000570701576 .

Ch. 9:

Lanier, pages 107-108

Conclusion:

Cheney

Washington, Conclusion

Acknowledgements:

Rogers, Fred. "Fred Rogers Acceptance Speech - 1997." *YouTube,* uploaded by The Emmy Awards, 26 March 2008, youtu.be/Upm9LnuCBUM.